FROM JOBLESS TO AMAZON BESTSELLER

MARC REKLAU

From Jobless to Amazon Bestseller. Copyright ©2015, 2020 by
Marc Reklau, Maklau Publishing Ltd.
All rights reserved.
Cover design by Vikiana
Printed by CreateSpace, an Amazon Company

Without limiting the rights under the copyright reserved above no part of this book may be reproduced in any form or by any electronic or mechanical means including information storage and retrieval systems, without permission in writing from the author. The only exception is by a reviewer, who may quote short excerpts in a review.

Disclaimer

This book is designed to provide information and motivation to our readers. It is sold with the understanding that the publisher is not engaged to render any type of psychological, legal, or any other kind of professional advice. The instructions and advice in this book are not intended as a substitute for counseling. The content of each chapter is the sole expression and opinion of its author. No warranties or guarantees are expressed or implied by the author's and publisher's choice to include any of the content in this volume. Neither the publisher nor the individual author shall be liable for any physical, psychological, emotional, financial, or commercial damages, including, but not limited to, special, incidental, consequential or other damages. Our views and rights are the same:

You must test everything for yourself according to your own situation talents and aspirations. You are responsible for your own decisions, choices, actions, and results.

Marc Reklau

Visit my website at www.marcreklau.com

"Don't wait. The time will never be just right."

Napoleon Hill

CONTENTS

Foreword..9
Introduction..17
I - The Myths, the Bad & the Ugly..........................**25**
II - Before You Get Started....................................**33**
  1.   The Obstacles You'll Meet..33
  2.   The Four Common Mistakes 37
  3.   Getting Started..39
  4.   Principles...40
  5.   The Big Idea..41
  6.   My Approach...43
III - The Beginning..**45**
  7. Why Self-Publishing? Why Amazon?........................45
  8. How to Start Writing..47
  9. Your Audience..51
IV - Your Content..**53**
  10. Will You Write Your Book?.....................................53
  11. Does Length Matter?..55
  12. While Writing..56
  13. The Outline...58
  14. Figuring Out Your Outline......................................61
  15. Before We Go On..63
V- Things That Are Crucial for Your Sales..............**65**
  16. The Title..65
  17. How I Found the Title for My Book 30 Days..................67
  18. The Cover..68
  19. Pricing Strategies..70
  20. Things That Didn't Work for Me..............................73

VI - Pages and Other Things to Set Up 75
21. Facebook Fan Page 75
22. Web Page 76
23. Opt-in Pag..e 78
24. Merchant Account 79
25. Newsletter 80
26. Autoresponder 81

VII- The Last Steps before the Upload 83
27. Find an Editor 83
28. How to Find an Editor 85
29. Format Your eBook 87

VIII- Upload Time! 89
30. Your Book Description 89
31. Choose Your Categories and Choose Them Wisely 90
32. Keywords Sell 92
33. Amazon KDP 94

IX- Bring Some Traffic to Your Webpage 99
34. Organic Search 99
35. Pay per Click 100
36. Affiliate Programs/JVs 100
37. Articles, Guest Blog Posts 101
38. Social Media 101
39. Using your book to generate Leads 103

X - The Big One: Your FREE Promotion 105
40. Your Free Promotion 105
41. Bookbub 106
42. First Things First 107
43. Three Weeks Out. 108

XI- The Aftermath..**113**
44. Secondary Strategies...113
45. Apple Books..114
46. Smashwords or Draft2Digital..114
47. ~~Createspace.~~ KDP Print..115
48. Audiobooks..116
XII- Conclusion **119**
About the Author..**125**

FOREWORD

I met Marc at a radio show where we were both invited to discuss the almost unlimited options to create wealth in this era. Right from the start, I connected with him. I think we both have a similar mentality centered on making effort, self-confidence and passion for what we do. I instantly knew that I had gained a friend and a fellow professional with whom I would definitely collaborate in the future.

And here I am writing the foreword to this book that he wrote and that I recommend you read.

Marc is an amazing coach and an exceptional person. Marc is one of those people who does something and then explains it to everyone who can benefit. He's not of those who speak from hearsay or unproven ideas; he does not sell hot air. He's "my kind of person." Both of us only give advice that has worked for us. When something works for us in any way, we don't keep it to ourselves. There are no kept secrets; we tell everything. Sharing is beautiful because abundance is unlimited for all of us.

In this book, Marc will guide you step by step on how to become a self-published author—a very interesting option in this era where intermediaries are disappearing gradually and the author reaches out directly to the reader, with complete control of his work and how it is shared with his audience.

You can do the same. We are in the era of indie or freelance authors.

The good thing about this era is that there are no excuses, no limitations. Anyone can do what Marc has achieved, and even more. The only way to make it happen is to stop talking about it and start doing it. This is why the author keeps on saying throughout this book, "You must start now, because there is no better time than the present moment."
Don't start tomorrow or the day after or next Monday! It is better to start the day before yesterday.

In this book, you will find all the resources you need to get help in creating and editing your book in both digital and paper-on-demand. The links are accurate; if you don't want to check each of them out, at least pay attention to the essential ones. It's where you will see that editing is simple, and so is fixing a price and selling your books.

This is not a boring, weak, technically convoluted book. On the contrary, it is a very practical manual that is to the point, does not make false promises, is realistic, and will show you a way that the author has learned from experience and research and has adopted in his own life. He has summarized this for you in an hour or two of reading. Isn't that wonderful?

I leave you with the author, Marc, knowing you're in the good hands of a humble, wise and very reliable person.

Happy reading!

Raimon Samsó, author of 14 books and 14 bestselling e-books on Amazon

www.raimonsamso.com

Malta, November 2020.

It's been five years since I first published *From Jobless to Amazon Bestseller*. A bit more than year ago, I did my first live workshop and went through the online course and noted that lots of things have changed in the self-publishing world. I've also made a lot of mistakes and learned a lot since then. Last but not least, I multiplied my monthly sales by 20 since 2015, so I figured it was time for a revised edition, so here we go.

Most of the things I mention in the books still work, some opportunities aren't there any more (free promotions don't seem to work so well anymore, unless you get tens of thousands of downloads), but some new opportunities came up, and I'm now earning more than ever before and making a full-time living with my books, thanks to paid ads. Right now, I earn about ten times as much per month as in my former job. British crime author Mark Dawson just made close to two million bucks in royalties last year (2019)—a whole bunch of it thanks to Facebook ads and Amazon ads.

I've also gotten rejected by even more publishers, gotten fired by an agent (I fired her right back), stopped working with my other agent and sold over $100,000 of international rights in the last couple of years. I've had various days selling over 500 ebooks a day and a couple of days selling over 1200 (thanks to BookBub, which still rules, but it is also more difficult than ever to get a featured deal).

While building my career as a writer only on BookBub featured deals didn't work out (they are just too difficult to get nowadays), I now earn more than ever, even without a BookBub deal, thanks to Amazon ads.

I've built my email list to over 10,000 subscribers just to lose over 70% of them again due to the new European data protection law in 2018. No harm done. Most of them didn't open their emails anyway.

I've been in the top #10 in the time management genre in the US Kindle store for over two years and #1 in the self-help genre in the Spanish Kindle store for four years, and I was still struggling financially, which makes me question a lot of the "6-figure authors" out there… and my spending behavior!

Strangely, most of these 6-figure authors sell a lot less books but seem to make a lot more money. This can happen for three reasons:
1) They make their money by coaching, speaking or consulting, and they use their book to get clients.
2) They don't earn their money by selling books but by selling courses on how to sell more books (which they obviously don't apply themselves).
3) They are lying.

In a recent blog entry, Amazon CEO Jeff Bezos states that there are over 1000 authors who make six figures on the

KDP platform. This is a surprisingly low number when you consider all those who claim to do so, and there are over 8 million books on Amazon.

A little tip: The authors who really make money on Amazon right now show you recent screen shots of their sales and not screen shots from 2015 or 2013.

Anyhoo...you can earn a living with your books, and many people do. These successful authors have some things in common:

1) They self-publish
2) They have many books (at least 5+, mostly 20+)
3) They work hard
4) They promote their books continuously
5) They pay for advertising
6) They keep on learning and improving
7) They are patient; this is a long game
8) They network with other authors

Right now, I have 14 books in English (including 2 workbooks and two 2 box sets), 13 books in Spanish and five books in German. I notice that the more books I have, the more money I earn, which seems logical.

Another great player is audiobooks. While at a round table I attended last year, two "publishing experts" said that audiobooks have no future and are very expensive to produce, but I have sold close to 20,000 since the beginning of 2019, and I never paid more than $500 for an audiobook production (check out findawayvoices.com).

My audiobooks bring between $300 and $500 a month, and that amount continues to grow—not bad for a product that has no future.

It's the best time in history to become a writer and to publish your book, so let's get to it!

I hope this books helps you. I'm not holding anything back, and I'm sharing everything I know. Anyways, don't only listen to me. Read more books on self-publishing. My go-to peeps are Mark Dawson and his podcast *The Self-Publishing Show*, Joanna Penn, David Gaughran, Derek Doepker, Nick Stephenson, Dave Chesson (the kindlepreneur), Brian Meeks and many more.

INTRODUCTION

In my first book, _30 DAYS: Change Your Habits, Change Your Life_, I wanted to take away all your excuses to not have a happy and fulfilled life and to give you the tools and exercises to become the master of your destiny and to create the life you always dreamt of.

In this book, I want to take away all your excuses for not writing the book you have inside you (I know you do!), or for not finishing that manuscript that is halfway done, or for not publishing your finished manuscript. Instead, I want to empower you to publish your book, and give you the tools and tricks to publish your book, market your book and hit it out of the park, just like I did in April 2015.

I'm going to tell you everything about how I got 40,000 downloads in 72 hours and how my first book literally took me from **jobless to bestseller (I wrote it while I was jobless)** and made me 12K in 12 weeks!

It's going to sound cliché, but trust me when I say, "IF I CAN DO IT, YOU CAN DO IT!"

I'm going to share everything I learned on my self-publishing journey—the good, the bad and the ugly. It's based on my experience of writing, publishing and marketing a non-fiction book.

Though this book mainly outlines everything that works for a non-fiction book, you should also find valuable nuggets for writing fiction, with the exception that I have no experience in outlining a fiction book, character development, etc., but I do know how to get over 300,000 sales and downloads on Amazon.

This book is a result of two years **[2021: 7 years]** of hard work, countless training modules and sessions I underwent, including reports and e-books on "how to be successful with your e-book," which I read till well into the wee hours, and the first-hand trial-and-error methodologies.

And the bottom line is that there is no sure-shot formula. What worked for me was a mix of what I learned during the training, what I took away from the reports and e-books and what my personal experience taught me.

Or it could be the simple belief that it's possible, **plus some kind of magic**, which I can only explain through reiterating Paulo Coelho's words: "If you have a dream, the universe conspires in your favor."

The only thing I always kept during the twelve exciting months between starting my book and my first more than 40,000 downloads on Amazon in 72 hours was my **BELIEF.**

I believed in my book, knowing I had created something great. With every positive feedback from friends after reading sample chapters, every free download, every 5-star review, every e-mail from grateful readers and every e-mail from publishers and agents, this belief grew stronger and stronger. And as the great Muhammad Ali once said, **"Once that belief becomes a deep conviction, things begin to happen."**

And indeed, things began to happen!

I hope this book will help you to develop a rock-solid belief in YOUR book too. I will also write a chapter about all the myths that I encountered and how I proved them wrong. And so will you! Just let that belief start to lay its foundation in your heart.

If you believe in your book and are convinced you have something good, you will ignore the haters, complainers, naysayers, doubters and scammers, and you will keep going, even if nothing seems to go in your favor.

Don't get me wrong—just believing is not enough. You do have to write a quality book and put in lots of hours of work. But you don't have to do everything alone. You write! When you are finished, you can get a freelance editor on upwork.com. It's their job to polish your book. They know how to do that.

Then you get a cover designer—somebody who formats your book for Kindle, etc. It's a lot easier than it seems!

It's surely a lot easier than it was in 2015, thanks to technical improvements and great formatting programs like Vellum.

I'm also writing this to show you that you don't have to necessarily do a coaching program worth $5000 to publish your book or pay a vanity publisher $2000 to $10,000 to make sweet promises and later leave you standing alone in the rain. Often these vanity publishers insist you buy one or two thousand copies of your book to get the ball rolling. You will meet many "experts" on the way who promise to help you publish your e-book and print-on-demand book for only $1500, $3000 or $5000.

If you meet these people, **RUN! RUN as fast as you can in the opposite direction!** You can upload your book on Amazon FOR FREE. They will also print your book-on-demand FOR FREE and pay you a percentage of the sales price.

You can get a quality editor and a quality cover for a relatively competitive price. [I paid around $250, most of it for the editor.]
I was poor (and jobless) when I started my writing adventure, so I had to invest time to find the best deals. Today, I'm glad I was poor, as I see how fellow writers have wasted thousands of dollars on things that don't work.

Do your research! Don't just listen to me. Do your research and listen to your gut feeling.

The approach in this book is for people who really want to **WRITE** their **non-fiction** book.
There are many other methods, which I will only mention briefly. I'll share with you what worked for me and hope that it will work for you too!

I'm sorry to say that this is NOT a guaranteed, surefire system! Just like every author is different, their voice is different, their work is different, and so is what works for them.

Seriously, if there was a guaranteed, surefire system, publishing houses would do a lot better and self-published authors would sell a lot more books.

Actually, 98% of authors, even traditionally published ones, never sell more than 1,000 books (I want you to become part of the other 2%).

Have in mind that at the end, it's still about trial and error. In the Kindle promotion, before "THE-ONE-THAT-CHANGED-EVERYTHING," I had only 699 free downloads in 5 days. I was doing nearly the same things that had brought me over 2,700 downloads some months before. In January of 2015, I sold a pitiful 8 ebooks in the whole month. I'm glad I didn't give up then because only 2 months later, I hit it out of the park. Well, more like BookBub's newsletter hit it out of the park for me.
As I said, I got 40,000 downloads of my book in 72 hours.

That's when it all started. You'll hear about this in detail later on in the book.

I also have to mention that I only have experience on Amazon. I never got my book on Apple iBooks, Smashwords, Draft2Digital, or Publish Drive, although those are great services. Maybe in the future I will. **[It's 2021.** *I tried to "go wide" with one book. It's still wide. Made me 100 bucks in a month. Now it's making 10. My other books are locked in exclusively with Amazon again. I'm very happy with them.*]

There are probably people asking a lot of money from you to put your book on Apple iBooks or Google Play. Smashwords and Draft2Digital (I love them, and their VP of operations Dan Wood is an awesome guy!) do that for you FOR FREE.

I'm not affiliated with fiverr.com in any way, but you will hear a lot about them in this book, because I just love that platform.

For $5, you can outsource most of your work to experts on this website. You can get things like logos, book covers, book trailers, book formatting, editing, book descriptions, etc.

There are a lot of people talking bad about Fiverr and considering it a horrible platform. That might be their experience. I've been working with them problem-free for six years now. It's all a matter of doing your research right.

There are also a lot of people who claim to be experts on self-publishing and on making lots of money. Do your homework. Check them out. If they are not in top positions on Amazon—and I mean in the whole store, not in some super hidden niche category—they are not selling many books.

So dive in! And above all, HAVE FUN!

I
THE MYTHS, THE BAD & THE UGLY

Before we really get started, let's do away with some myths that could keep you from writing, or in the worst case, not even allow you to start your adventure.

The Myth:
Who are you to write a book?
The Truth:
Who are you not to write a book?

The Myth:
It takes a lot of time to write a book
The Truth:
I wrote my book *30 Days* in 3 months, and the book you are holding in your hands I wrote in under a month. (With a little more discipline, I'd have had it finished it in two weeks.)
In a time when the attention span is getting shorter and shorter, and people get more and more distracted, a short informational e-book might be a winner. I recently read that Spanish author Alex Rovira wrote his book *Good Luck* in eight hours. It sold over 3 million copies.

The Myth:
When you self-publish, it means you don't have enough credibility to get a traditional publisher.

The Truth:
There are so many examples of self-published authors being contacted by traditional publishers. Actually, I'm one of them. I was contacted by two publishers directly and by one agent. My fourth book, *Destination Happiness,* was published by Spain's #1 publisher. *Fifty Shades of Grey* was self-published first.

I was contacted by a small US publisher even before BookBub hit it out of the park. I've even read about self-published authors rejecting 6-figure publishing contracts, because they wanted to be in control of their book! With a traditional publisher, and for 10% of the catalogue price, you lose control of your book.

There are already horrible stories of people who sold many e-books until they signed with a traditional publisher and after that, they received NADA, ZERO, ZIP.

This happens when the publisher doesn't know the tricks about pushing e-book sales with the right price or in the right category. They don't know the ideal price point for e-books and sell them nearly as expensive as physical books. Or you might be one of 50 authors he is juggling, and you may be further down on his list of priorities.

[**2021:** *I'm a self-published author, yet I published one book with Spain's #1 publisher PLANETA and sold international rights to more than fifteen publishers around the world and counting. In Spain last year, four self-published authors I know got contracts with traditional publishers. But remember, the book that was published with a traditional publisher is my least-selling book. Another thing: all the rich authors I know are self-published and all the traditionally published authors I know are poor.*]

The Myth
You need a literary agent.
The Truth
I would love to have had a literary agent at the beginning of my career! Too bad I was ignored by 10 or 12 of them (maybe more!). I wasn't even rejected like bestselling authors J.K. Rowling, Jack Canfield, Stephen King and many more. I was simply **IGNORED**.
Maybe that was luck. The good thing is that it didn't stop me. I just put up my book and started doing free promotions. Then I got contacted by a Korean agent. And then a Turkish agent picked up my book. Then I started talking with a Polish agent, and somehow I think with my book on 50,000 Kindle readers, mobile phones and tablets, this is only the beginning.

I had the luck to know a very good lawyer who checked my contracts in the beginning. (Thank you, Irene Abad Mayor!)

[2021: *I just broke up with my my second agent. The first one fired me, and then I fired her right back. I sold 80% of my international rights by myself. My books have been translated in over 15 languages. If I can do it, you can do it. If you sell a lot of books, foreign publishers will contact you. I learned that if I ever work again with an agent, I won't give them exclusive rights. I have no problem paying them 20 -25% of the contracts they bring, but it's very frustrating to pay that kind of money to them for contracts from publishers that contacted me first. Anyway, once you get a contract offer from a publisher, it's better to talk to a specialized lawyer or an agent and have them take a look at it.*]

The Myth:
Managing editors of publishing houses only talk to agents, not to authors.

The Truth:
Not if you know someone who knows someone. And you probably do...
Think six degrees of separation—some people even say it's only four. Thanks to friends, I talked to the managing editors of two major publishing houses in Barcelona. They didn't pick my book up for other reasons, but I did talk to them.

The Myth:
Publishing doesn't work like this anymore. Publishers don't look for you and don't pay advances any more to publish

your book. **You pay to get published.** "If you chose Rocky Press (invented name) as a publisher, we will make you a star. Louise House (invented name) signs one or two of our authors every year." (Yeah right! What they didn't say is that you have to invest 1,000 to 10,000 USD.)

The Truth:
This is the biggest bunch of crap! Thank god I read a horrible article about a certain vanity publisher some days before their call. They play with the emotions of people who want to have their books published, take their money and then give nothing back—at least that's what you can read online…but don't listen to me whining. Do your own research!
Think of it this way: if I paid you 5,000 USD in advance, what incentive would you have to make my book a success? You already have your money.
A serious traditional publisher who pays you an advance of 3,000 or 5,000 USD or more will surely have a bigger incentive to sell your book to make their money back.

I told the vanity publisher, "No thanks! I'll give the old way a shot and won't pay for somebody to publish my books!" And even if nothing would ever have happened with my book, it became a winner right there! Because in the end, I saved a lot of money by ignoring such "offers."
About a month later, I was contacted by my small publisher who paid to publish my book.

[2021: *This has probably gotten worse. Many players on the playing field who make big promises take your money and deliver...NOTHING! If you follow the people I mentioned, it won't happen to you. Dave Gaughran is especially good at pointing out the scammers among us. Follow him and listen to him.*]

The Myth:
Once you have more than 50,000 downloads, 59 reviews, an average 4.6 out of 5-star rating, more than 3,000 sales in 10 weeks, sell the book to two publishers and have two agents looking out for you, you have achieved amazing results that nobody can dispute.

The Truth
Someone will come up to you and tell you that your book is not good enough, that people are not interested, because "with this number of downloads, you should have more reviews." Don't listen, don't bother, just do your thing!

I listen to everybody's advice. But in order for me to take it seriously, it has to come from somebody who has produced something and has sold more books than me.

Would you take advice on what to do in your marriage from a divorced person? Or advice on how to invest your money from a guy who is bankrupt? I wouldn't. (Except maybe if they said, "Do the opposite of what I did.")

Secondly, when the phrase ends with, "I can help you fix it if you pay me xxxx USD," which most of the time is the case, I lose interest.

Actually I would go so far to tell you to run from anybody who asks for a high sum of money in advance!
My lawyer takes a commission.
My agents take a commission.
My publishers pay me advances.
My Spanish editor worked on commission.

See a pattern?

To make a long story short: **Don't let any of the above hold you back!**
Your job is to write, publish, market, market, market and market some more. And believe in your book! And relax. And learn. And adapt. And fall. And get up. Don't ever listen to the doubters, the complainers and the fear mongers. If somebody tells you, "You can't do it," prove them wrong!

In the meantime, write another book.
[**2021:** *I don't read my reviews any more. There's always somebody mean around. Paulo Coelho's The Alchemist has 627 one-star reviews and J.K. Rowling's first Harry Potter book has 261 one-star reviews. On social media, for a long time, I fed the trolls, defending myself, explaining. Now I'm using a better method. It's called DELETE and BLOCK.*]

II
BEFORE YOU GET STARTED

1. The Obstacles You'll Meet

Let me warn you right in the beginning:
You will definitely be deterred from writing your book by at least one of the five biggest obstacles. And they might creep up over and over again throughout the journey:

- **Confusion** ("OMG, I have no idea where to start.")
- **Overwhelm** ("I have no time right now." "I have so many other things on my plate.")
- **Procrastination** ("I'll start tomorrow.")
- **Fear** ("What if people don't like my book?")
- **Doubt** ("I'm not an expert." "I'm not a writer." "Who am I to write a book?")

Face them. Observe them. **But don't let them stop you!** Be aware of them and send them away if they show up. Fear and doubt might always be at your side (they were at my side all the time and still are).

Just one week before publishing my book, fear and doubt hit me right in the gut. I panicked! Suddenly, I started doubting my work and doubting my editor, and I didn't like my book anymore. In my coaching training, I learnt that fear and doubts in most cases are imaginary; you have to look for facts. So that's what I did.

1) I went back to the elance profile **[*2021:* now upwork.com]** of my editor: 5 stars, great comments. Okay. No reason to doubt her.

2) My book. I loved every chapter of it over the three months of the writing process. I got great feedback from people who read sample chapters. No reason to doubt it now.

The facts were on my side. So it had to be fear, baseless and imaginary fear (which by the way makes for about 90% of all fears we feel). Anyway, I still went on and hit the "save and publish" button on my Kindle Dashboard **despite** the looming doubts and fear.

It's actually no coincidence that all those fears and doubts crept up just before publishing. It was my mind's last effort to keep me in my comfort zone. **[2021: It still happens to me every single time I hit publish.]**

That's how we are wired. We like the familiarity of the comfort zone. It's comfortable, and we know what happens next. But what will NOT happen in the comfort zone is growth and development. Your book won't get written either. If you don't get out of your comfort zone, you are STUCK, my friend, and the worst thing is…you might not even notice.

So face the fears and doubts, and publish anyway. You'll get feedback on your book soon enough, and if you write it from your heart, put your soul into it, and write it to help people, I can bet the feedback will be positive. I guarantee you that! Don't believe me? Go ahead and prove me wrong.

2. The four common mistakes, and how to overcome them

The 4 common mistakes unsuccessful authors make:

1) They don't have an overall book strategy.
2) They think everyone is their ideal reader.
3) They write without a plan.
4) They isolate themselves.

What can you do to *not* fall into that trap?

1) Strategize your book.
Don't just start writing your book. Take 30 minutes, and answer these questions NOW! It will make everything easier. Usually the first answer that comes to mind is a good one. Write that down before the negative self-doubting voice overpowers them.

What do you want the book to do
- For yourself?
- For your readers? For me, this was the most important question.
- For your business? More income? Attract customers?
- For the world?

Who is your ideal reader?
Who is it most important for you to help?
What problems do they have?
What pain can you ease for them?

Develop a writing plan
Make an outline. I cannot emphasize the importance of this! It will save you from both not being inspired and from writer's block.

If you can't make it alone:
Get support
Support makes the impossible possible. It eliminates the four biggest obstacles!

You can get support from a coach, from your friends and family, and even from other budding writers.

If your goal of writing and publishing is big enough, you won't need any support from the outside. Your goal in itself will give you the drive that makes you jump out of bed in the morning to start writing and to find the time you need to write everywhere!

3. Getting Started

Okay then! Are you ready for this? Let's do this! As Plato already said, "The beginning is the most important part of the work."
It's important that you work at your own pace. I recommend you consistently do something every day to create momentum.

And my dear...let me make one thing very, very clear:
There are only two reasons why you won't finish this writing project.

Reason number 1: You lose your DESIRE to do it
You can avoid this by always remembering:
What motivated you to write your book?
Did you want it to be a source of income? Or a credibility tool?

Reason number 2: You lose the BELIEF that you can do it
Remember, you can do it!
There are many tools to build your belief. You can use affirmations, visualizations, meditation and many more.
I highly recommend you write down your goals and stick it somewhere you can see every day—maybe right next to your mirror. If you're serious about this, you will find an entire collection of tools in my book _30 DAYS: Change Your Habits, Change Your Life_.

4. Principles

Stick to the principles I share with you in this book. Replicate the steps of someone who has made it. Which, by the way, is exactly what you are doing if you follow this book. You will replicate the steps of someone who has made it, who in turn replicated the steps of many who have made it.

I'll also put up a list of all the resources that I used <u>on my website.</u>

Begin with the end in mind. Remember what we talked about under the point "Strategize Your Book"?

Don't let perfectionism hold you back! Don't worry about the details. You can go over those when your manuscript is finished.

For now, **WRITE!**

A good idea is to **commit to a date; it's even better if you do it publicly!** I posted on Facebook and in my newsletter that I would have the book done on June 30, 2014. That was in April 2014, when I hadn't written a word.

It helped: the manuscript was ready on the 30th of June. After editing and polishing (and a vacation thrown in between), I published at the end of August.

5. The Big Idea

So what's the BIG IDEA for your book?
Are you going to write about your own story? How you achieved a goal? About your knowledge of a certain topic? **Helping or solving a problem for your readers is a winner, and the "how to"/DIY category is always a good category!**
If you are not sure about what to write, you can check forums/social media/blogs on what's moving people.
My advice is to write on a topic that you are already familiar with. There is something about going through the pain to understand your readers' mindset and to empathize with them.

Think evergreen! Your book should be timeless so readers can pick it up ten years from now and still connect with it. Check the following for ideas:
- Amazon
- Facebook
- Reddit
- Quora
- Magazines
- YouTube

Write down your ideas as they come.
Write or think about it from the following perspective:
It's not what you think they need; it's what they really need!

Think niche. Some best-selling authors on Kindle "write to market," which means they first look for a profitable niche, research it and then start writing about it. This is a smart idea because they are writing about something that people are already searching for.

On the other hand, nobody cared about vampires or wizards before the Twilight or Harry Potter series came out.

I'd recommend a mixture of two approaches. If you want to write about your passion, investigate if there is a niche for it. If there isn't and you want to write it anyway, just go for it! Maybe you'll create a new niche.
Just remember, **it's not what you think they want to read; it's what they really want to read!**

People who want to make money on Kindle write various books in various niches, and that's another good option.

6. My Approach

WRITE WHAT YOU'RE PASSIONATE ABOUT
Writing about your passion comes with the following advantages:
- You already know a lot about the subject.
- You speak the language of your readers.
- You know where to find your readers.
- It fuels your DESIRE.
- You write from the heart, which is the best way to connect with your readers. They will feel your authenticity and get to know your voice.

WRITE THE BOOK TO A PERSON YOU LOVE
One year after starting it, I noticed for the first time that I actually wrote my first book to my younger self. Fifteen years prior, I was a guy who had read loads of self-help books and had loads of knowledge, but I never actually applied that knowledge or did the recommended exercises, so I stayed stuck for quite some time in a job that I didn't like. I had relationships that were not healthy, and I was practically lost, because I never took 15 minutes to find out what my true values were. I never wrote down my goals. Once I started DOING the exercises, EVERYTHING changed.

Action step:
- Write down at least 10 ideas to research first, and see which one you identify with most.

III - THE BEGINNING

7. Why Choose Self-Publishing? Why Amazon?

There are two options for getting your book out there: self-publishing or traditional publishing. They both have advantages and disadvantages. Self-publishing offers some really great advantages over traditional publishing.

1. **Your royalties are a lot higher:** 70% or 35% from Amazon against 8% to 10% from a publisher. In the printed book business, agents, publishers and distributors take their cuts; plus, you have to add the production and material costs. Self-publishing can be done with very little money. Amazon KDP now also prints on demand and gives you a much higher percentage (60%).

2. **As a self-publisher, you keep complete control** over your book. The cover, content, keywords, categories and last but not least, prices are entirely up to you.

3. **It's so much faster** to get your book self-published. Finding an agent, then a publisher, then getting your manuscript read and approved can take years.
When you self-publish, you can get your book on the market in a matter of weeks.

For me, it was clear that instead of waiting to be discovered or accepted by an agent or publisher, I wanted to take my destiny into my hands and get my book on Amazon as quickly as possible. While I was dreaming of getting discovered, I continued working hard. With time, opportunities came up. The harder I worked, the more opportunities came up.

WHY AMAZON?

Amazon has a market share of 41% of all new book purchases, 65% of all new online book units (print and digital) sold, and 67% market share of e-books, and it controls 64% of sales of printed books online (according to *The Wire* as on March 2014). **[2021: I suppose these numbers have grown considerably, but I'm too lazy to research. Sorry.]**

They also have the data of millions of credit cards ready to buy at 1-Click. People can download your e-book with one click.

8. How to Start Writing

You're going to need FOCUS and DISCIPLINE! If you don't have these two character traits, it will be very difficult to finish your book, because you won't run out of excuses for procrastinating.

Do you have a ritual for the first 30 and last 30 minutes of your day? If not, now is the time to develop one! Here is what I wrote about the importance of rituals in my book *30 DAYS*:

THE MOST IMPORTANT HOUR...
The most important hour of your day is composed of the thirty minutes after you wake up and the thirty minutes before you fall asleep. This is when your subconscious is very receptive, so it's of big importance what you do in this time. The way you start your day will have a huge impact on how the rest of your day develops. I'm sure you have had days that started off on the wrong foot, and from then on, it got worse and worse. Or maybe the opposite happened, where you woke up with that feeling that everything would go your way, and then it did. That's why it's very important to begin your day well. Most of us just get into a rush from minute one after waking up, and that's how our days unfold. No wonder most people run around stressed nowadays. What would getting up half an hour or an hour earlier every morning do for you?
What if instead of hurrying and gulping down your breakfast or even having it on the way to work, you get up and take half

an hour for yourself? Maybe you even create a little morning ritual with a 10- or 15-minute meditation session. Do you see what this could do for your life if you made it a habit? Here are some activities for the morning ritual. Give them a shot!

- Think positive: Today is going to be a great day!
- Remember for 5 minutes what you are grateful for.
- 15 minutes of quiet time.
- Imagine the day, which is about to start going very well.
- Watch a sunrise.
- Go running or take a walk.
- Write in your journal.
- The last half-hour of your day has the same importance! The things you do in the last half-hour before sleeping will remain in your subconscious during your sleep. So then, it's time to do the following:
- Write in your journal again.
- Reflect on your day. What did you do great? What could you have done even better?
- Plan your day ahead. What are the most important things you want to get done tomorrow?
- Make a to-do list for the next day.
- Visualize your ideal day.
- Read some inspirational blogs, articles, or chapters of a book.
- Listen to music that inspires you.

I highly recommend that you do NOT WATCH THE NEWS or MOVIES that agitate you right before going to sleep. This is because when you are falling asleep, you are highly receptive to suggestions. That's why it's a lot more beneficial to listen or watch positive material. The planning ahead of your day and the list of things to do can bring you immense advantages and save time. The things you have to do will already be in your subconscious, plus you will get to work very focused the next day if you already know what your priorities are.

Questions:
1) How will your mornings and evenings look from now on?
2) Will you get up 30 minutes earlier and develop a little ritual?
3) What will your last activity be before you go to sleep?
4) After your morning ritual and before doing anything else, spend 15/30/60 minutes on your book project. Block this time and **put it in your to-do list the day before.**

If you are an evening person, that's when you should sit down for an hour and work on your book.

Make it a habit! Write a little bit every day!

Even if you write "only"100 words a day, in 6 months, you will have 18,000 words! And you don't have to be a genius to write 100 words a day. You just need to have an outline and be committed. Yes, it really is that simple.
I started writing every day at 6:30 in the morning till I had at least 1000 words or until at least till 9:00. But often, I wrote and researched till noon without even realizing that it was noon.

I wrote 8,800 words of the book you hold in your hands right now in 3 days! But that was based on the notes I had taken throughout that year.

9. Your Audience

Some questions you have to ask yourself are the following:
- Is there an audience for your idea?
- Will they pay for your information?

It's research time again:
Check Amazon for keywords and for books with a high number of reviews. Check the Amazon bestsellers' lists (they change every hour) and category rankings.

If you hit the Top 10,000 PAID category, you will sell quite a lot of books.
You don't need to reinvent the wheel! No matter what niche you want to write a book on, know that many people, when looking for information, buy multiple books on that subject.

If you don't know what to write about, check what people are searching for on the internet. You can also check magazines, Facebook, etc.

Don't think too much either. Don't over-analyze your idea. ACT ON IT!

If your first idea doesn't work, try another one.

Action steps:
- Develop a ritual.
- Use at least 2 or 3 tools to confirm the marketability of your idea.

IV - YOUR CONTENT

10. Will you write your book?

Here is an important question: **Will you write your book?**

Many people who earn money on Amazon actually outsource the writing process to **ghostwriters** and have many different books under many different pen names spanning many different niches.

There are also people who **speak** their book. They tape themselves and later find a freelancer to transcribe it into a book or transcribe it themselves. Dictation programs keep getting better and better.

I chose to write my book myself, because my belief is that if you put your heart and soul into it, the readers will notice, and your book will become successful. (Yup, I'm that kind of an idealist and a hopeless romantic.)
You could hire a ghostwriter, or you could license it. There is something called *resell rights*; you need to go through this in detail if you want to go down this road.

You can also take a book that is in the public domain. That means there's no copyright on it. You could either sell it on your home page or on Amazon (be careful: Amazon has some strict rules on the subject) or even give it away for free on your webpage to collect subscribers. **Walt Disney built an entertainment empire with this trick: He took old fairytales from the public domain and made movies from them.**

11. Does Length Matter?

What's the best length for a non-fiction book? There is actually no rule of thumb. It depends on what it takes to convey the information. It doesn't have to be a full book. But if you want to have a chance to get in the BookBub newsletter, the minimum is 100 pages.
Fifteen thousand to 20,000 words is a good length. My book *30 Days* has around 39,000 words. Somebody even said it's too long. My other books have around 25,000 words.

I have seen books on Amazon that are around 30 to 60 pages and maybe 5,000 words. I'd go for a minimum of 15,000 words. **[2021: My two last books are 14,000 words long. Most people like them.]**

The most important thing is the information and the value that your book provides.
If you write a shorter book, you need to WOW your readers with the content, but if you are unnecessarily lengthening the book with fluff or writing in a font size of 16 or 18 just to squeeze some more pages out of your book, your readers will notice it, and you'll lose credibility.

12. While Writing

Don't be a perfectionist! Remember one thing:
DONE is better than PERFECT!

Don't let anything distract or block you. Turn all your devices and notification sounds off! Your job is to write. Don't edit your chapters while you create. WRITE. Later, you can find an editor whose job is to make your writing look nice. They are trained people. You just need to WRITE.

Remember, you're not trying to win a Pulitzer Prize.

You're conveying information. Robert Kiyosaki, the author of the bestseller *Rich Dad, Poor Dad*, said it best: **"I want to be a bestselling author, not a bestwriting author."**

All that said, your writing should fulfill the minimum and basic rules of the language you're writing in. Don't make your editor work too hard!

As I mentioned before, I highly recommend you hire an editor. That's an investment you should make, because it is definitely is worth it. There are good people on upwork.com, and you can also find editors on fiverr.com.

I outsourced to an editor from Upwork (Gisela) and was totally happy with her. This book was edited by Mawra Ishaque, who is also a genius.

OK…just one more step before you start writing. This is the most important one. I can vouch for it.

This will keep the dreaded writer's block at bay. Once you do this, there will be no dearth of inspiration.

You won't get stuck!

Okay, okay, here it is:

13. The Outline

Without this "trick," I'd never have finished any of my books.

If you sit in front of a white computer screen waiting for inspiration to hit you, it's not going to happen. Inspiration isn't a stroke of genius. You can find inspiration in anything BUT not every time. Staring at the white MS Word page is terrifying, and chances are, you might never get any further than that with your book.

It actually happened to me a month before starting this book. But then I thought, "How did I start *30 Days*? Right...I outlined it!"

Starting to structure the book and outlining what I wanted to write about took me about 2 days. You can use mind mapping or just write down what you want to write about.

Thanks to this, I never once suffered from the feared writer's block or from a lack of inspiration!

I put some time in the outline, and I had about 106 points I wanted to write about. I decided to make a chapter on each point.

I opened 106 folders in Word and wrote the chapter's title on top, and then I closed all the pages.. I created 2 more folders and named them "Finished chapters" and "Chapters to-do," and by then, I knew I wanted to write a minimum of 300 to 500 words per chapter.

Then I started writing.

When I wasn't inspired to write one chapter, I went to the next one. When a chapter wasn't finished but I couldn't think of anything else to write, I archived it in the "Chapters to-do" folder and moved on to the next. With time, the folder titled "Finished chapters" got fuller and fuller, and the folder titled "Chapters to-do" got emptier and emptier.

To have an overview, I created an Excel sheet with all the chapter names and word count of each chapter, and I highlighted the finished chapters.

I wrote the introduction last!
(I wrote the introduction of the book you are currently reading when I was already more than half done.)

Believe me, once you hit 12,000 to 15,000 words, you won't stop any more, no matter if you are inspired or not.
You have come too far, and it feels too good.

I think it took me 6 weeks to write the first 25,000 words and another 6 to write the remaining 14,000 words of *30 Days*.

But by then, I was unstoppable. In the last week before finishing the manuscript, I deleted 8 chapters, because by then, I really wasn't inspired anymore, and it was taking me longer and longer to write each chapter. I also already had 90% of the book done, so the 90% became the 100%!

The reason why a lot of authors fail is because they face this problem right at the beginning of the book, and they never get to finish the book.

Put some time into strategizing the outline of your book. It will be worth it!

14. Figuring out your Outline

You are probably thinking, "Hey, Marc, I get that an outline is important, but I have absolutely no idea how to do that." I didn't either, so I did some research and like I said, my own trial-and-error methods helped.

Here's a simple procedure:
First of all, I recommend you read at least 4 to 5 books on your subject to get an idea of what you want to write, both from a macro and micro point of view.
Second, take a look at their Table of Contents and see if you get any ideas for your own Table of Contents. Then I would go to Amazon and check out another 5 to 10 books on the subject. Amazon allows you to read the first 10% of the book in their "Look inside" feature, so use this to get a clearer idea for your Table of Contents. Important: listen to your intuition; it's usually right!

A very raw outline would look like this:

Introduction
Chapters
Subchapters
Summary
If you put enough time into your outline, you will have the skeletal framework of your book.

THE CHAPTERS

Put the chapters in order, and give each chapter a compelling title. Your chapter titles should be like little headlines to draw the reader in. Your chapter titles sell the chapter!

A way to do this is:
Write 20 things you want to write about.
Cut that list down to 10, and put them in chronological order or put them in a natural/logical order.

As I said before: write, don't edit.

Now that you have your chapters in order, you need to start writing! In *30 Days,* the chapters are very short and could have been in any order. I actually put the chapters in order last, and I might even change the order in the future.

As I mentioned, you should have your chapter titles by now, but don't worry, you can always change the titles until the end. WRITE!

Another question you should have in mind is whether you will put assignments/action steps at the end of each chapter.

15. Before we go on

Remember the following things:
- Create a habit of writing!
- Avoid distractions while you are writing (turn off e-mail and text notifications, put your phone on silent, turn off your social media and YouTube).
- Write every day. Thirty minutes should be possible for even those stuck in challenging jobs.
- Set a word count goal (1000? 500?). Even if you only write 300 words a day, that means in 60 days, you have an 18,000-word book. Sounds like a pretty big number, doesn't it? You start small, but over time, you can see your efforts culminating into something bigger.
- Don't get distracted. Don't let anything stop you.
- You don't have a title for your book yet? No problem; it will come. There is time!
- You WRITE! Don't edit! I didn't read what I wrote until I had 15,000 words. Once you have 15,000 words, you won't stop anymore.
- **Don't be a perfectionist!** Write! The editor can improve your text once the manuscript is finished.

Many people never finish their books because they are such perfectionists and are just never happy with their chapters, so they stay stuck on the first chapter and never move on because it's just not good enough.
- Remember: **DONE is better than PERFECT**
- Get rid of the belief that it takes very long to write a book! Vic Johnson teaches how to finish writing a book in ONE

weekend! Wesley Atkins's new program teaches you to write an e-book and get it on Amazon in 7 days!

I know of people who have finished books in less than two weeks. The important thing is that the quality doesn't suffer.

V - THINGS THAT ARE CRUCIAL FOR YOUR BOOK

16. The Title

The title will be an important part of your marketing. It's true that your book will be judged by its cover. It's said that 50% of the time, people choose or don't choose a particular book based on the TITLE. So you better write a killer title.

Hint: The same formulas that make good headlines make good titles.

And don't forget that the title and the subtitle are also good opportunities to put in some keywords, but don't exaggerate. [Actually, as I'm writing these lines, I still have no idea about the title of this book. All I know is that it will come to me with time.]

Good titles make a promise, pique interest, talk to people's needs or simply give a sneak peek to the book's content. You can also name a problem and offer the solution as your title.

HOW TO FIND YOUR TITLE
- Check magazines or newspapers for the most read, most commented, and most recommended headlines.

- Look at books in bookstores and check which titles catch your eyes.
- Go back to the Amazon bestsellers' lists and check which titles sell.
- You can also synthesize titles, which means you take titles of successful books and adapt them. For instance *The 7 Habits of ..., The Power of...*
- You can also ask your friends, conduct a survey or leave it to your intuition.

Just don't let the fact of not having a title stop you from writing!

Here are some examples for titles:

101 Ways to...

How to..

Eliminate...

Avoid...

7 Steps to....

13 Ideas for...

The Art of...

The Truth about...

The Key to...

...include words like *magic, secret, stop,* etc.

My friend Derek Doepker has a great course called "Books That Sell." You can find it on the resource page.

As I already said, don't get too obsessed with the title, and **don't ever let it block you from writing!**

17 .How I found the title for my book 30 DAYS

I only had a working title for my book and decided to just write. I even sent the manuscript to the editor without having a title! Once I sent to the editor, I knew I had about one week to find a title, and I knew it would come to me. I didn't know how, and I didn't know when. I only that it would come.

On Sunday, July 13, 2014, the day of the FIFA World Cup Final, I went for a great lunch with my friends Inma and Pol at a beautiful place on the island of Ibiza with great views. And then, after a great lunch and a bottle of white wine and some coffee with some alcohol in it, it came to me: ***30 DAYS.***

I don't recommend this technique for finding a title nor do I want to encourage you to find your title at the bottom of an empty bottle of wine. All I'm saying is that it will come to you, so don't let the lack of a title stop you from writing the book.
The most important thing is, as always, to **keep on writing!**

Action step:
- Write down 20 possible titles for your book, even if they sounds stupid. (DON'T SKIP THIS. IT'S IMPORTANT.)

18. The Cover

People will judge your book by its cover. Period. So this is one of the things where I'd advise you to invest some money. Even if you are—or think you are—a great cover designer, outsource the cover design to a pro. You'll be surprised by their perspective and the final result.

There are experts who will charge you 200 USD to 500 USD or more for a cover design, or you can go the route I took: I ordered three Fiverr gigs. One knocked me off my feet. That became my cover. Investment: $15.
Browse a little bit on fiverr.com. There is a lot of great talent.

Other places to find a cover are **99Designs** or **Freelance Cover designers.**

FIVERR.COM
Before I go on, I'm going to tell you a little bit about how I use Fiverr.
I use it for a lot of jobs, so here is how I go about it. It takes a little time, but it's worth it:

- Browse on what you want (e.g., cover design, editing, e-book formatting, etc.)
- Go to "High Rating" if you want the absolute best, or you can hire someone newer too if their portfolio samples look great.

- Check out the sellers.
- Usually I look at the ones with lots of positive reviews.
- Check how many bad reviews they have and what people say about them (yes, read the reviews!).
- I made Excel sheets to see their good/bad reviews at a glance, percentage of overall reviews, how long they need to deliver the job.
- Then buy.

Or sometimes, I just go with my gut feeling.

Back to the Cover…
I only got a flat version done, which is enough for your Kindle e-book. If you want to get fancy and get a 3D cover along with a Facebook header, keep some money aside since it'll go over the $15 mark. I did the Facebook header myself with this great, free online design tool at canva.com.
Take into account that the full-size of the cover doesn't show up on the Amazon page. It's only a thumbnail. People should not only be able to read the title but also find it attractive. You have to make it stand out. Experiment with the contrast and different colors to **make it POP!**

19. Pricing Strategies

Now the fun really starts…talking money!

BAD NEWS first: If you are not a well-known celebrity, you probably should keep the price under 5 USD!
Amazon pays the maximum royalty (70%) between $2.99 and $9.99.
Any other price will only bring you 35% royalty.

Here's what I learned:
Use $0.99 as a promotional price around 7 to 10 days before your free promo.
Make sure your book is at least $2.99 the day before the free promo on Amazon starts.
[You can also put it for $4.99 or even at $9.99. Amazon will then mark it as $0.00 instead of 9.99$ at the day of the free promo which looks like a great deal. Who doesn't want to download that book?]

After your free promo, play around with the prices again: Some people leave the book on $0.99 for some days to get some additional exposure. On the last day of the promo, put your price to $0.99 if you want, or $2.99.

Smashwords did a study and found out that the sweet spot for many readers is between $2.99 and $3.99. Amazon has a fantastic gadget "Buy with one click." It's just like that: you click once and your e-book gets delivered to your Kindle reader or your Kindle app. Pricing up to $2.99 seems to be the sweet spot where people still download with one click by impulse and don't think too much. I had the book on $3.99 and $4.99, and one reader even told me it's too cheap...but at the price of $2.99, I sell the most copies.

[2021: *Nowadays and thanks to Amazon ads, I have nearly all my books priced at $4.99, and it works fine for me. If you advertise on Amazon, that should be the price, as with a price of $2.99 or $3.99, you might not make a profit, and you may even lose money, but of course other things also influence the sales, like your cover, your description, reviews of the book, etc.* **]**

A couple of years ago, I also found out that $1.99 as price point doesn't work at all. The Smashwords study found that out many years ago. I found it the hard way when I got no sales on a $75 ad. That's money down the drain. It was disheartening, but it happens.

Of course, you will also have to skim through your competitors' pages and check what price range they have resorted to. Pricing is just a thing you have to play around with a little.
Listen more to your intuition than to me, and try different things and adapt!

[2021: If you are a new author, you should definitely offer some books for $0.99 or even free promotions to get your first thousand or so readers. I don't do free or $0.99 promos any more. I'll launch at $2.99 and then raise to $4.99. That's because I worked hard and have an email list of 18,000 people and because Amazon ads take care of the rest, even with a book priced at $4.99.]

MORE THAN ONE BOOK? TRY THIS:
If you have more than one book, there is a very interesting pricing trick that many authors who have already tasted some success with their e-books on Amazon apply.

They price one of their books at $0.99 or even for FREE while the other book is at a slightly higher price. This brings them a lot of traffic, which results in more downloads [a Smashwords study in 2014 found that free e-books are downloaded 39 times more than priced e-books], and most of the time, the sales of their other books that are priced at $2.99 or $4.99 go up too.

If you want to give away your book for free on Amazon, you either have to do a free promotion and give Amazon 90 days of exclusivity (you can't sell your e-book anywhere else then). Or you make it "permafree," which means you upload your e-book to Smashwords, price it at $0.00 and tell Amazon to "price match."

Action Step:
- Set your price!

20. Things that didn't work for me

...but you can try them if you want...

BOOK TRAILER
Do you want a book trailer? Forget about it. I made one bit it had **ZERO impact on my sales.**]
Here's the one I released in August 2014:
https://youtu.be/6hCz44a-IuA
And this is the updated one from May 2015:
https://youtu.be/144YkQJ89cA

If you really want a book trailer you'll meet the same pattern: You can pay somebody $100 to $150 to get a book trailer done. Or we yet again go to our favorite place, Fiverr, and get it done for $5. I went to Fiverr, but you guessed that already.

I had to buy the music and video rights though; otherwise, YouTube blocks your video. That was another $50, but totally worth it.

Make sure you include the dates of your free promo, or at least the month when it's up for free download.

ARTICLES

You also should create some articles from your book or pay somebody to write them. **[This is something I didn't do.]** You could send your book to a ghostwriter and tell them to write 15 to 20 articles about topics from the book.

PRESS RELEASES

Create some press releases. There are templates available, or get somebody on Fiverr to do it for you.

I did the press release myself and then got three different Fiverr gigs to distribute it on about 30 free PR webpages.

[Full disclosure: On my most successful Kindle promo, I didn't use press releases and haven't used them since]

Ok. So by now you have written your book, found a title, and gotten a cover designed.

ANY PR or MARKETING SERVICES

Don't even think of it. It's a total waste of money and you'll never make the money back. I've heard horror stories of people investing thousands of dollars and then selling only 26 books.

Don't do it! If you don't believe me, do your research.

Before we go on to get your book formatted and uploaded on Amazon, let's look a little more at marketing. You've got to be prepared when the big day of your promo comes.

Action steps:
- Create your graphics, articles and press releases.
- Create your book trailer.

OR DON'T - IT WON'T MATTER

VI - PAGES AND OTHER THINGS TO SET UP

21. Facebook Fan Page

Man! Creating a Facebook fan page was something I procrastinated for months, always thinking it would be so complicated. But when I finally overcame that block, I set it up in 5 minutes. Yes, 5 minutes. It's really easy! Name the Facebook page after the book or just adapt your professional page a little to focus on the book. Have a look at mine here: http://www.facebook.com/marcreklaucoaching
If you plan to write more books in the future (I really hope you do!), I suggest you go with your name +author for the Facebook fan page.

Anyways, **in 2021** due to the low organic reach of Facebook fan pages, mine is totally deserted. When I first wrote this book, the organic reach of fan pages was around 60%. Now in 2021, it has gone down to 2-3%. I just use it to run Facebook ads every now and then. This is actually a pattern I observed with a lot of self-published authors. But of course, it's up to you. Keep in mind: You need to have a Facebook Fan page (a.k.a. Business page) if you ever decide to do Facebook ads.

22. Webpage

Having a website is a must. I just added a book page to my website www.marcreklau.com and made it the landing page (home page).

If you want to be fancier, buy the domain name of your book. Buy the .com if it's available. It's a common thought among people who deal with websites that if you have the .eu, .net or anything but the .com address, they will think: "Look at the poor devil. They can't even get the .com domain (which usually costs a bit more); they must be really strapped for cash!"

- If you use your name or the book title as your domain name, make sure it's easy to remember.
- The shorter the better.
- Avoid hyphens and special characters in your domain name.
- Make it as easy as possible for people if you tell them your web address over the phone or if you are mentioning it on the radio later on.

Optional:
There are services where you can build your webpage or find somebody who makes a WordPress webpage for you.
You can also do one of the many free tutorials that are available. You choose! If you have a lot of time, you can choose to work through it all by yourself. If you are pressed for time, outsource to a freelancer.

You're using your webpage to market your book, so you need the following:

BLOG

Write something at least every 2 weeks (the more often the better) and build an audience. But work consistently, because there is no bigger put off for your fans and clients than an abandoned blog! (I found it a lot more beneficial to write more books than to write a lot of blog articles.)

[2021: *My blog is totally abandoned. I change the dates of the blog posts every now and then. That's it. Still selling tons of books, so I guess blogging is not that important.*]

23. Opt-in Page

That's where people leave their name and email address and in return get your newsletter. Nowadays, it's quite difficult to get people to subscribe to your newsletter or to get an email address in exchange for nothing, so what most people do is offer a free report, videos, a free e-book, etc.
[I offer some free coaching worksheets to the readers of *30 Days*.]

If somebody offers me their free "e-book" for download and I get 8 pages with a font of 22 and 1000 words, I hardly consider that an e-book. Instead of adding credibility for me, it takes away credibility. For something like that, I would rather go with "free report."

Once you have a domain for your webpage, you need a webhost, one that makes it easy to install WordPress. For example, HostGator or GoDaddy are the most common ones. As I went with Vistaprint, who did all that stuff for me, I have no idea how to get that all done. For me, that's like Chinese. You will have to talk to an expert or do some research on your own, or (surprise surprise) you could also find somebody on fiverr.com who will get the job done for you.

24. Merchant Account

After you create your webpage, get a merchant account. I recommend PayPal and set up a shopping cart or an e-store if you want to sell your book from your webpage.

I let Amazon handle all that for me. They have far better shipping tariffs than I'll ever get from any courier or mailing service, plus they handle everything.
If a book gets lost, or is delivered late, they take care of it.

At the beginning, I made the books available on my webpage, but I soon found out that it's less of a headache for me and cheaper for my readers if I let Amazon handle it.

It's WIN-WIN-WIN: I earn three bucks less per book but have absolutely no worries. My readers get far better prices, because Amazons tariffs with couriers are just very good, and then Amazon gets their share.

[2021: Lots of new options here. If I wasn't exclusive with Amazon, I'd look into www.payhip.com where you can sell your e-books directly to your readers.**]**

25. Newsletter

Ok. So now that you have your webpage set up, I recommend you sign up for a newsletter service. This is absolutely crucial, although it has been said that email is dead, but it's working better than ever for me. Also experts say, **"Don't build on other people's real estate,"** which means Facebook, Twitter, LinkedIn or Instagram can close your account or just go away and what happens then? Yup. All your contacts gone.

Have you ever noticed how the world's biggest social network, Facebook, gets in touch with you? Yes, email. Makes you think, right?

I now use and warmly recommend mailerlite.com. I used to use mailchimp.com, which is free up to 2000 subscribers. Aweber.com is another option.

That's what you use to build your subscriber list. You can create opt-in pages that you then embed in your webpage or Facebook fan page. Or you send people directly to the opt-in/landing page you created with your newsletter program. These are great programs where you put all your contacts' email addresses. You use it to send your newsletter weekly or at least twice a month.

A little piece of advice here: Don't try to sell something with every newsletter. Give information, free stuff, tips and maybe do soft selling every four newsletters. People don't like the idea of being sold, even those who are looking to buy. Your aim should always be to form a relationship with them, gain trust and then see if your product fits their requirements. You'd not only get more business but also repeat business.

26. Autoresponder

Now the best thing: The **AUTORESPONDER!**
This is a programmed email sequence of follow-up messages that are automatically sent after somebody downloads your free gift. You do it once, and all your future subscribers will get a sequence of 8, 10 or however many emails you want automatically. You can program it, for example, Day 1 after download: "Welcome again…blah blah blah." Day 5: "How is it coming along? Did you like the free report?" Day 8: "Can I help you in any way? Please let me know." Day 15: "I found that product. I really love it; what do you think?" etc. etc. etc.

[**2021:** *These are all great tips. but to be honest, the only thing you need are a webpage and an email marketing service like MailChimp to set up your email database and lead magnet, to collect subscribers, for a landing (opt-in) page, for newsletter campaigns and for autoresponder. Yes, the email marketing programs do all this now for a relatively low price compared to what all this cost 5 years ago.*]

Action step:
- Implement at least 3 of those suggestions. You will thank me later. :-)

VII- THE LAST STEPS BEFORE THE UPLOAD

27. Find an editor

You have finally finished writing you book! Now it's time to find an editor.
I recommend upwork.com; although, there are also lots of people on fiverr.com.

Delivering your draft to the editor is one of these moments when doubt hits you full in the gut, and for most authors, this is the perfect moment to procrastinate and get distracted.
[It happened to me then, and it's happening while writing the draft of this book again]
[2021: It still happens to me with every freaking book!]

You might think "the draft is not ready yet," "There's something more to do," "Maybe I should include that chapter I was thinking about," "Maybe I should delete the entire book and stop stressing!" **Forget it!**
Find a good editor and turn in the draft. It's the editor's job to make your book better! They will come up with suggestions to improve the book, so even if you think it's not that great, you can turn it into a bestseller. But remember, you can only improve upon something that exists, so start writing!

There are two forms of editing: content editing and copy editing. Get an editor who can do both!

Content editing is about the flow of your book: does the overall idea flow sequentially, are there any chapters you have to develop, or did you include too much fluff? Is there something that should be more pronounced, clearer? A content editor does an overall job of packing and processing the content of the book while keeping your tone, idea and writing style intact.

Copy Editing
Once the content editing is done, the editor goes deep. Everything from grammar to spelling to sentence structuring is scrutinized and (if required) rectified. The editor also helps with wording and verbiage and gives suggestions to improve the overall content.

This is essential work. Too many grammar or spelling errors might get you bad reviews and annoy your readers, which in turn will hurt your sales numbers significantly!
As I said before, hiring an experienced editor is a worthy investment.
REMINDER: Don't do any formatting yet! Do the formatting after the editing process is finished.

28. How to find an Editor

As I mentioned before, I looked for an editor on upwork.com It's a little more expensive than fiverr.com, but in my experience the freelancers, Upwork are very professional.

It's quite easy to do: sign up, post a job, and watch the offers pour in.

Here is my job posting in the category **Writing & Translation > Editing & Proofreading:**

"Proofread and Edit Personal Growth eBook
I'm looking for an experienced proofreader and editor (native English speaker) to edit and proofread my 34,000-word manuscript and to make sure the grammar, spelling, syntax, punctuation, capitalization, etc. are correct. Any suggestions that can make the book better are welcome."
I got around 80 offers for that posting. So I checked the reviews, stats and work samples, and I narrowed down to 10, then to 5. I renegotiated with 3 freelancers and followed my gut feeling giving the job to Gisela.

You can even interview people or call on Skype. I based my choice on reviews, writing and editing samples, price and the duration of the job.

Some more things to take into account:
- Make sure the editor understands that there is a deadline (no more than 2 weeks, in my case).
- Have in mind that you'll go back and forth with the editor 2 to 3 times; that should be enough. Don't use this as an excuse to procrastinate! By now your fears and doubts should be at their worst! It's normal, and it happens to the best of us. Don't let this stop you.
- He or she should have work experience on a book like yours.
- Clear communication with deadlines, tone of the book, and budget.
- Pay a fixed price for the job.
- Get an editor who is experienced in both copy and content editing.
- Make sure the editor uses track changes in Microsoft Word so you can see every change made. You will have to approve or deny these changes.

Once that is done...

Congratulations! You now have the final version (for now) of your e-book ready!

Let's move on to e-book formatting.

29. Format Your e-book

Make sure you are done with the editing process first. Don't format your e-book until you have the final, edited version of your book, because it's better to format for ePub once you are sure of the editing and have the final version in hand.
Ok. Then let's get to it!

It's formatting time. You want to get your MS Word doc ready for uploading on the Kindle platform. I think by now, you have discovered a pattern:

1) You can do it yourself keeping in mind all the rules that Amazon has for
   Kindle-Formatting. This will probably take a lot of time. Here's the <u>link</u> if you want to try anyway.

2) You can search on the internet for Kindle formatting and compare prices from "experts," which are between $100 and $150.

3) Or, you can use <u>fiverr.com</u>.

Guess what I did—I paid "bookaholic" on Fiverr $5 and got my word document formatted. She is my go-to person and an absolute pleasure to work with. **[2021:** *Unfortunately, bookaholic stopped working on Fiverr. My go-to guy now is Serhio Goncharo, who also does an amazing job. Amazon rolled out their own tool, which is called Kindle Create. It* *gets better and better. You just upload your Word doc, design a little and then get your finished file to upload on Kindle.*

Some authors use a program called Vellum and love it. I finally started using it, and it's great.]

Have in mind: If you have photos, bullet points, tables, etc., the price could be a little bit more, because those are a little more complicated to format.

Action steps:
- Find an editor.
- Get your draft edited and polished.
- Convert your e-book into Kindle format.

[2021: *Things have gotten a lot easier these days, and there are many places where you can get your book formatted for free. Draft2Digital has a formatting program on their site, Reedsy, and Amazon came out with their own tool called Kindle Create. Most of the authors I know use and love VELLUM (Mac only), and soon my friend Dave Chesson (the kindlepreneur) will have another amazing tool out.]*

VII- UPLOAD TIME!

30. Your Book Description

Woohoo! Exciting times! You, my dear friend, have finally completed your book, you have it edited by a great editor, you have your cover designed, and you have your webpage, Facebook page, mail program and maybe even your autoresponder setup. Great work!
You are now ready to upload your e-book on Kindle! And it takes less than an hour...

You will save time because you will get to the upload page prepared, so before going there, do the following:

- **Write a 200- to 400-word description (or hire a freelancer if you want at Fiverr).**

[Remember: You just wrote a book of 10,000 or more words. I think you can write a description of 300 words, can't you? Of course you can! Just write it from your heart.
I wrote my book description from the heart. One day, I didn't like it any more. This was probably because I had read too many articles on "how to write the perfect book description," so I changed it. I wrote one following all the super tricks and tips...and my sales dropped! Two days later, I put my old description up again.]

31. Choose your keywords and categories, and choose them wisely

- **Choose 7 Keywords:** What words would people use to find your book?)

- **Choose 2 different categories,** not 2 different subcategories of the same category.

[Your chances of being found by potential readers are much bigger if you choose TWO different categories!]

BAD:
 Self-Help > Self-Esteem
 Self-Help > Motivational

BETTER:
Self-Help > Self-Esteem
Business & Investing > Time Management.

MORE ABOUT CATEGORIES:
You want to be included in the following categories:
Avoid a category if the top 5 books have a best-seller ranking of 40,000+. There is not enough traffic coming to this category, and it's not a popular selling category.
You want to look for a category in which the top 5 books have best-seller ranks around 20k and preferably a couple of books under 10k. That's a category that sells!

Category Checklist: Cover these 4 points as well as you can.
1. **The category is relevant to your book's topic (duh!).**
2. **Select 2 different categories.**
3. **Top 5 books of the category are ranked in the top 20,000 overall and better.**
4. **The top 3 books in the category are ranked 2,000 or worse, AND the top 2 books are ranked 15,000 or better.**

This is what I wrote about keywords in the original version of this book. Truth is, I lost my belief in the 7 keywords Amazon lets you choose. I don't know if they sell a lot of books. What I do believe in are the hundreds of thousands of keywords I'm running ads to, because I can actually see how many impressions they get (=how many people see them), how many people click on them and how many sales each keyword makes. So you can read it or skip it. For me, it's not valid any more - for many people it is, so I didn't want to erase it.

32. Keywords that sell

When you think about keywords, you should think about how your readers will search for your book!

One of the ways to find keywords is to **type the keyword into the search bar on Amazon and see what suggestions come up** (the most-used terms).

- The keywords should be related to your title and subject of your book.
- Check the top left corner for the number of titles using your keyword.
- If you get more than about 750 results for your keyword phrase, you'll probably be better off trying a different search phrase.
- The top-ranking book should have a sales ranking of around 10,000 or better.
- Also, check out the book number at the bottom of the page. What's its rank? If it is ranked in the top 10,000, it's very difficult to compete with this keyword and get on page one of the search results (which should be your aim).
- If most of the books are ranked in the 50,000 or worse, there's not enough traffic for this keyword, so move on!
- If there are four or five titles ranking in the 10,000 range, then the keyword is probably getting traffic!

Another way is to come up with a list of possible keywords, type them into the Amazon search bar and check what Amazon offers, and if they meet the criteria mentioned above.

Investigating keywords and categories is a lot of work. I use a fantastic tool called KindleSPY, **which does all the research for me. The time you save already pays for it!**

[2021: This was the old way. I personally don't believe in the 7 keywords anymore, as I have over 330,000 keywords working for me in my Amazon ads. If you still want to find your best 7 keywords, you better check out my friend Dave Chesson's tool Publisher Rocket, which is also great for Amazon ad keywords.]

33. Amazon Kdp

ISBN

Amazon KDP Print and Smashwords require an ISBN number. You can buy those for yourself or get them for free (Amazon). I got mine from Amazon because I really did not want to pay $125 for one ISBN number.

Enroll the book in KDP Select. That's where the magic happens!

This enables you to do 2 types of promotions:
1) The Free Book promotion
2) The Kindle Countdown Deal.

[*2021:* *Although these promotions have lost effectiveness, I just don't dare to take my books out of KDP Select. There are rumors that KDP Select books are treated better by the algorithm and you need to be inscribed into KDP Select to get Amazon Prime Deals. Amazon Prime Deals are the bomb. This means your book will be made available for free to Amazon Prime Members. Now you might think that this will harm your sales. Well…it doesn't. It even boosts your sales because you get so much visibility. I don't know anybody who was harmed by a prime deal, so if you want my advice, say yes if you get offered one. Another nice side effect of prime deals is that I get 50 to 80 new subscribers PER DAY when my book has been chosen for a US prime deal.*]

But beware. The condition of being in KDP Select is to give Amazon **exclusivity for 90 days** to your e-book, which means that you cannot sell it anywhere else.

Not on your webpage, not on Smashwords, not on Apple, nowhere.
Anyway, the exclusivity is for your e-book only. You can still sell your paperback book wherever you want.

Okay, let's start! You'll have to put in the following information:

- Title
- Is the book part of a series
- Description (copy and paste your prepared text)
- Author
- Language
- Publication date
- Verifying your publishing rights (confirm that you have created the book and hold the copyright)
- Categories (put your two researched categories here)
- Keywords (copy and paste your 7 researched keywords here)
- Upload your cover
- Upload your book file
- Preview/save
- Verify your publishing territories (you want to put worldwide here)
- Choose your royalties (70% or 35%)

- You can set the price automatically on the USD price or you can put it manually (I have cheaper prices in India and Mexico)
- Allow lending (half of my royalties comes from lent books)
- Save and publish!

Woohoo again! You did it! In a few hours, your book will be LIVE on Amazon! Amazon says it takes 24 to 48 hours; with my books, it actually always takes 6 or 7 hours [except for once, when there was a technical error].

As you are already setting up things, why not go right to **Amazon's Author Central.** You should have your author page at least in the US and the UK:
authorcentral.amazon.com
https://authorcentral.amazon.co.uk
https://authorcentral.amazon.de

Put your picture and a small biography (back cover of your book). You can put your book trailer and connect the page to your blog and Twitter feed.
Share your author page with your friends and share it directly from the author page.

Now is also a good time to buy some blog posts on fiverr.com and to ask your friends for reviews of your book. **(The KDP free promotions should be like 3 weeks out.)** You might send review copies of your book to reviewers [I didn't do that yet] and buy some Fiverr gigs like "post a message to

100,000 Twitter followers"- send the link of your bookpage [mine is http://www.amazon.com/dp/B00N2GDB0K].

Don't forget, if you are new, it is better to hire people who have high ratings, and make sure to go through reviews to see there aren't many bad reviews.

ATTENTION:
DO NOT USE FIVERR OR ANY OTHER PAID SERVICE TO GET BOOK REVIEWS POSTED AT AMAZON (or any other retailer). If you get caught, you get thrown out of the Kindle store, and your publishing adventure stops here, or at least it gets a lot more difficult!

~~Get 5 to 6 legitimate, honest reviews from your friends, colleagues and family. That should do it for starters~~.
[2021: It's now also against Amazon terms to get reviews from friends and family, so I advise you to not do it. (The only way to get legitimate reviews is to sell or to give away many books.)**]**

Action steps:
- Upload your book
- Create your author page
- Build links to your book
- Get 5-6 reviews [sell or give away many books!]

IX - BRING SOME TRAFFIC TO YOUR WEBPAGE

Now that your book is uploaded and the day of the big promo is nearing, let's get some traffic to your "author platform," which is your social media presence, your web page, your blog, YouTube, etc.

This can be done in the following ways: Google, Pay-per-Click, Affiliate Programs or Joint Ventures, Articles or Guest blog posts and last but not least your social media activities.

34. Organic Search

- Google is the main player!
- The algorithm changes too fast to worry about it.
- Think simple. If it's good for the visitor, it's probably good for SEO!
- Use a good SEO plugin for WordPress.
- Create lots of quality content.
- Create lots of social interaction (Twitter, Facebook).
- Use an incentive to get FB likes and comments ("Like this and get a surprise bonus").

[2021: All this didn't work for me at all. **]**

35. Pay per Click

You have Google, Bing and Facebook. [I only used Facebook with little success.] If you use these, change your ads frequently to avoid "ad blindness."

Start out small and track your ROI (return on investment). If you pay $20 and make $25 in sales, you actually earn 25 cents for every dollar invested. If you make only $15, you're losing money. STOP!

Test - Test - Test.

[2021: Amazon Advertising and BookBub ads have become real game-changers. Organic traffic got very low on Amazon, and based on what I see, the authors that really earn a lot of money with their books are highly invested in Facebook ads, BookBub ads and Amazon ads. Mark Dawson's online course *Advertising for Authors* was life-changing for me and increased my sales twenty times over. You can check it out on the resource page. The course only opens twice a year.]

36. Affiliate Programs/JVs

- You might need higher-priced products to attract JV partners and affiliates. This comes into play when you have your online training program or workshops.
- Become a valuable affiliate, and you will attract JVs.
- Grow your audience.
- Find products you like.
- "I've been in your affiliate program for quite some time and want to appreciate…"
- Do something for them ("I wonder how I could help you").

37. Articles, Guest Blog Posts

This is where the articles you created in Chapter 5 come into play.
- Locate some blogs in your market or niche.
- Evaluate the strength of the blogs by checking how many people like, share and comment on their posts. You can also put their URL into alexa.com where you will see which position the website is in worldwide.
- Contact the owner and send them your information: bio, link of your website, affiliate program and your best UNPUBLISHED article.

[**2021:** This didn't work for me. I'd advise you to spend your time on learning advertising than on searching guest blogs. If you know people who it worked for learn from them].

38. Social Media

Social media by itself is difficult to monetize, but its strength is unmatched visibility. Facebook has now over 2.6 billion users, YouTube 2 billion, WhatsApp 2 billion, Instagram over one billion. I'd say you have a pretty great chance of reaching out to a broader audience with these platforms.
Ask yourself this question: How can you get people to opt in? I'm working with Facebook, Instagram Twitter and LinkedIn. I don't know if I have ever sold a book via social media. Actually, I doubt it. But social media is a great way to be in touch with your readers and to show them a bit of who you are or what your writer's life looks like .

RECAP: I didn't do guest blogging or affiliate programs. What changed my life was Amazon advertising, and I highly recommend learning Amazon ads if you really want to start selling some books.

If you get into the BookBub newsletter (I'll take more about it in the next Chapter), all that becomes secondary.

It's extremely difficult to get on their mailing list, but once you do, the entire process becomes hundredfold easier and faster. You might not have to get PRs and blogs written, because you get a lot of the right traffic through them.

They have statistics that show you exactly how much traffic you can expect. For the Advice and How-to category in March 2015, that was between 8,500 and 27,000 free downloads. So I calculated with around 10,000.

On Tuesday the 31st of March, the day of the BookBub promotion, I got 36,842 downloads, and things started moving.

39. Using your Book to Generate Leads

To further build your author platform, you want to collect lots of fans, email-addresses, or as the sales people call them, "leads."

Every book should have at least one offer (a.k.a. lead magnet) in it! It should be relevant to the book topic and could be anything from a free book, a PDF, a complementary entrance to a live workshop or a discount to an online training. You can even use an affiliate offer if you don't have your own product.

Put the offer on one page in the beginning of the book and on one right at the end of the book. [I know it hurts and surely won't happen to your book, but some people actually don't finish all the books they start, so you want to have your offer in the beginning!]

Since I published my book, I have gotten over 700 new subscribers, and that's just for the coaching worksheets I offer. And I don't even include a special offer.

SALES FUNNEL

A typical product funnel in the personal development business looks something like this:

- Free report, video, worksheet or low cost e-book
- $49 to $69 audio product

- $297 - $995 home study course
- $4,997 VIP Day
- $1,997- $25,000 mentoring/coaching program

Action step:
- Use some of the tricks mentioned in this chapter to bring some traffic to your website.

X - THE BIG ONE: YOUR AMAZON FREE PROMO

40. Your free promotion

Everything I wrote before comes down to this! The way your free promo goes makes the difference between HERO and ZERO, SUCCESS and FAILURE! NOW IS WHEN THE RUBBER MEETS THE ROAD!

[Ok, ok...faaaaar too dramatic! It's just a free promo. If this one doesn't work out, you can make some adjustments and just do another one the next time you can. The second free promo, the one before the promo that led to 40,000 downloads in 72 hrs, I made a mistake and got only 699 downloads. I accepted my mistake and prepared the next promo a lot better.]

If you apply the tips of this book, your free promo should get at least 1,500 to 3,000 downloads. You might become #1 in your category in the FREE bestseller's list (actually you will be a BestGIFTER then), and maybe when your book goes back to the paid books list, you can experience a moment of glory in your paid category by becoming a bestseller for two hours in your category. [Take screenshots!]

Then you can call yourself a #1 bestselling author forever

after, like most of the #1 bestselling authors do before dropping back into the abyss. [FUN FACT: If you sell 150 to 200 books a day you probably won't care if they call you a bestselling author, because you actually are one.]

[2021: I built all my success on FREE promos. Unfortunately, they don't work as well any more to boost you rankings and your launch. Also, most of the free promo pages don't work as well any more. Nowadays, if at all, I work with 5 to 7 promo websites, and I pay them, while in 2015, I worked with 80 or 90, and they were all free… Today, I mostly do $2.99 or $0.99 launches and run a BookBub ad targeting myself towards the book, send a couple of emails to my list, and if I'm lucky, Amazon takes over. Thanks to Amazon ads, I get continuous sales of all my books and don't depend on launches anymore.**]

41. Bookbub

I applied to get on the BookBub newsletter 4 weeks before I had my free promo planned. They'll tell you within a week if you get featured or not.
Once I got the ok from BookBub **(not before! We don't want to mess up here! Remember to build your KDP free promotion around the BookBub promotion date),** I scheduled my free promo on my Kindle dashboard and took the date from BookBub as my third out of five free days to get a lot of momentum **[maybe the fourth day would have been even better].**

If you get into the BookBub.com newsletter:
CONGRATULATIONS! You ARE A BESTSELLING AUTHOR. You will get anywhere between 8,000 and 30,000 FREE downloads [that's what their statistics say, and I have no reasons to doubt them], maybe 40,000, and the next months will be some of the most exciting months of your life. And yes…you will sell a lot of books!

42. First Things First:

The free promo will bring you in front of thousands of new readers!
As I said, to enjoy the free promo, your book MUST be in the KDP Select program, which gives exclusivity to Amazon.
You'll get five days for a FREE or discounted promo in any 90-day period.
Go to the Promotions Manager in your KDP Dashboard and set the type and date of your promotion. [The promo starts at midnight Pacific Time.]
WRITE A PLAN before you start your promotion.

Have your book up at **least 2 to 3 weeks before the promo,** so you can get at least 6 reviews (the more the merrier) before the promo starts. [Remember to price the book at 0.99 cents.]

The video trailer you created in Chapter 5 should include your free dates. Upload the video on YouTube 2 to 4 weeks out and promote it via social media to create some expectation.

Get your Facebook fan page up as early as possible—even before your book is finished! Like...**NOW!** Put free promo dates on your timeline cover "Download FREE Copy at Amazon xx/xx - xx/xx." (Use canva.com to create it or outsource.)

Post chapters, exercises tips, and relevant topics on your Facebook page [I posted motivational quotes, which definitely helped].

43. Three Weeks Out:

IMPORTANT! SUBMIT YOUR FREE DATES to every single one of the 60+ FREE PROMO WEBSITES that will promote your book for you, or pay the six or seven webpages that still work and save yourself a lot of work.

[I like to be in control, so I submit to all the websites myself. It's lots of copying and pasting, but I'm particular that way. It took about 4 hours, but I did it myself, so I can't blame anybody if I don't get the number of downloads I wished for. I used ebookbooster.com once and had a terrible result, which I naturally blame on them without any proof, although it might not even have been their fault.

Warning: Some of the free webpages ask for a minimum number of reviews. You can also pay for a guaranteed spot [which I didn't do when I started out, but now I do].

SUBMIT YOUR PRESS RELEASES

...or pay somebody on fiverr.com to submit your press releases to some free PR sites. This should be done 7-10 days before your promo starts. Check on fiverr.com how long the seller needs to do the job (some need 7-10 days). That information is available for every seller. Set the release date for the morning your promotion begins!

[**2021:** *I did press releases once. Never again. Skip them and save yourself some work.*]

YOUR CONTACTS

Notify everyone you know multiple times by multiple means that your promo will start soon.

FACEBOOK EVENT

Create a FB event (2 to 4 weeks out) to let friends and friends of friends know, and tweet a lot.

[**2021:** *Don't do it. In my experience, it just takes a lot of time and won't sell a lot of books.*]

ON THE DAY OF YOUR PROMO – TO-DOs!

- Post on Facebook and on your personal page that your book is for free today. Post three times a day.

[I always felt kind of strange and pushy when I was asking people to download my free e-book until I read this great quote from fellow writer Jeff Goins: "It's hard to be annoying when you're asking people to share something that is for free."]

- Buy a sponsored post on Facebook and show it to friends of friends to get some exposure. Do this over three days [I didn't get a lot of success from that, but it might work for you].

- Buy a Facebook ad and send it directly to Amazon or wherever you want. The link was always my problem because I always wanted to put links to 6 stores for my friends in 6 different countries till I found this amazing thing: http://relinks.me/B00N2GDB0K This link sends everybody directly to their country's Amazon store... AMAZING!

- Get your Twitter going in the morning and tweet multiple times over various days. You can program your tweets with Hootsuite. [I have obviously too much time on my hands, because I always tweet live.] **[2021: Nowadays, I don't even tweet any more. Seems like a waste of time to me.]**

- Go to Fiverr and buy some gigs of people who are going to tweet your book to hundreds of thousands of people or post on FB [I personally don't know how effective this is, but some authors swear this has worked for them.]
- Continue your posts, tweets and all promos for three days, and if you're applying everything you learnt in this book, **at the end of the second day, you should see some results that will make you very happy.**

- There are also websites that promote your book for free on the day of the free promo. Submit to them now!

- Check your rankings and take screenshots! You probably will hit #1 in your category and call yourself #1 bestseller from then on. [You are actually a BestGIFTER, because your book is still for free.]

If your promotion worked, the momentum is now driving your book in the rankings! Enjoy every second of it! I was glued to the Amazon screen, taking screenshots for days. It's a fabulous time!

If you didn't make it into the Top 10 Free list for your category, figure out what happened, check your category (maybe it was too competitive), learn, adapt your strategy, write another book and go again in 90 days! [Remember my BIG DAY came on the third promotion after half a year of trial and error!]

XI - THE AFTERMATH

44. Secondary Strategies:

Congratulations! Your book is on Amazon. You uploaded it. You hopefully had a successful launch, hit the bestsellers' lists and your e-book is now in the hands of thousands of readers!

But hold on! You are not done yet.
Actually, the real work starts now. You have to keep on working, tweaking, hustling, and marketing your book. It took me 6 months of consistent work after publishing to finally get my breakthrough.

TIME FOR SECONDARY STRATEGIES!

At this point, the only other REAL player in e-books is the APPLE iBookstore. If you are not doing Amazon KDP Select, you should definitely get onto Draft2Digital. Some authors even go directly to the other platforms and get on all the other e-book stores.
Draft2Digital will do that for you FOR FREE. Don't pay anybody a lot of money who tells you to do this. It's for free! Pay somebody on Fiverr to format your e-book for Draft2Digital (or do it yourself), and then upload it [I'm still exclusively on Amazon. Before my free promo of April 2015, I played with the thought of leaving. I'm glad I didn't.]

45. Apple Books

APPLE ADVANTAGES:
- In the iBookstore, you have far less competition than Amazon.
- Apple is more sensitive to keywords and great covers.
- Great international coverage.
- They allow you to give away 50 promo copies (think reviewers…).

46. Smashwords or Draft2Digital Advantages

If you don't want to do all the work, use Smashwords or Draft2Digital. It's a one-stop distribution to Apple, Barnes & Noble, Sony, Kobo, libraries and more, plus it's one of the few Apple aggregators (they get commissions from Apple and then pay you). They provide a free ISBN number and keep a relatively small commission of 10%. As I said, they also convert your book to all formats for free.

[2021: *I'm still exclusively on Amazon and loving it. I think I could never have built my business the way it is without being exclusively on Amazon. But that's only me. Some people have ethical or moral concerns when it comes to Amazon. I can only tell you that everything I own is thanks to Amazon. When nobody wanted to know anything of me, I got the chance to upload my book and take destiny into my own hands. Another example: In the COVID-19 crisis, when many companies used the crisis as an excuse not to pay me,*

Amazon was paying punctual every single month so I could compensate the non-payments of other clients. That's ethical to me.]

47. KDP Print

MUST-DO: GET ON KDP Print! (formerly known as Createspace)
Everything has gotten even easier because you now manage ebooks and paperback books from your KDP dashboard.

This is a must-do: Get your PAPERBACK book out there as soon as possible!
[2021: I just recently uploaded my print books (Paperback and Hardcover versions) also to Ingram Spark so that I can even reach more people. Many libraries and book shops that don't want to buy from Amazon can get my books via Ingram]

You can send your interior part to a person who lays out print books for $100 to $150. You might find somebody on Fiverr who does it at a very good price, or you can do it yourself, like I did! It took some time, but I felt comfortable doing it myself. In 8 hours, I got my Word document formatted as paperback (it's a PDF). Nothing fancy, but good enough.

My e-book cover designer also designed my paperback cover. She only needed the cover measurements (Amazon creates a sketch based on your page numbers, desired paper quality and measurements of your book.), text of back cover (book synopsis and author bio) and that's it.

This cost me $10.

Once you have your cover, you upload it together with the interior part to KDP, and within a week, you have your paperback book connected to your e-book on Amazon (probably much faster).

From that moment on, Amazon will also put "You save XX%" next to your e-book and compare your e-book price to your paperback price, which by the way is usually a lot higher. This should drive additional sales to you e-book.

[2021: Wow. Times have changed. While in 2015, most of my sales came from e-books; now over 60% of my sales come from paperback books.**]**

Once your books are up as e-books and paperback, start thinking about hardcover and large print. It's the same formula; more products means more income. It goes without saying that this only works if you have a good product.

48. Audiobooks

Audiobooks have become a force to reckon with, and their sales numbers are soaring! Another advantage is that there is still far less competition than in the e-book market.

Nearly all my books have audiobook versions. Some were produced by audiobook publishers; the rest I produced myself with a great company called Findaway voices.

Here's their website: https://findawayvoices.com

It's even easier than e-book production: You sign up for an account, look for a narrator, e-sign some papers, send the PDF of your book and on you go.

Yes, it's really that easy. If I was able to figure it out, you'll be able to do it, too. [Yours truly is not a great techie.]

Action steps:
- Get your paperback version on Amazon.
- Think about getting your audiobooks done.

XII
CONCLUSION

We are almost done! I hope you had fun! Do you already have plans for your next book? I hope you will get the same results I did!

It has been an amazing five years since "The-Free-Promo-That-Changed-Everything!"

Here is what my book did for me in the first 9 months since publishing, and in 3 months since "the-free-promo-that-changed-everything":

- More than 200,000 downloads and sales on Amazon. [That means I'm on over 200,000 Kindle readers, mobile phones, iPads and PCs. Seriously, who wouldn't want to be?]
- More than 3,500 e-books sold so far. **[2021: I can't even count any more, but I think in total, I'm north off 300,000 sales.]**
- Signed a publishing contract with a small US publisher for the Americas (Spanish language rights). **[2021: I have now signed over 30 foreign language rights contracts.]**
- Found by a Korean agent who sold the translation rights to a Korean publisher **[Big mistake. They don't pay me anymore. Cheaters!]**
- Signed a traditional publishing contract with Spain's #1 publishing group PLANETA **[not the success I expected]**.

- A Turkish agent is looking for a publisher in Turkey. **[2021: That didn't work out.]**
- A Polish agent will evaluate the book, and if she likes it, I will hopefully sell the translation rights to a Polish publisher. **[2021: That didn't work out, but I recently signed with another Polish publisher.]**
- Negotiated with an Indian publisher; unfortunately, we didn't come to an agreement. **[2021: Didn't work out, but I signed with an even better Indian publisher who managed to sell 30,000 copies of my books in a year.]**
- Translation rights of my books worth +$100,000 sold to over 15 countries.
- TV, radio, blog, podcast interviews.
- New coaching clients from all over the world.
- 700 new subscribers to my mailing list and counting. **[2021: Now 20,000 and counting.]**
- Loads of happiness. **[2021: If somebody tells you that money doesn't make you happy, go to social media and look at my smile.]**
- Loads of confidence. You walk and talk differently after 50K downloads. [Imagine how you walk after +300,000 sales, making five figures a month and six figures a year].
- It's easier to approach people for partnerships/JVs.
- People listen to what I have to say. [That wasn't always the case.]
- Amazon [Yes, the mighty Amazon] is promoting the Spanish version of *30 Days* right now as I'm writing this (July 2015). It's the #1 bestselling book in the category

Economy and Enterprise ahead of Pope Francisco and Greece's Ex-Minister of Finance Mr. Varoufakis and #9 in the Spanish Kindle Store overall. **[2021: I love Amazon; meanwhile, I've been #1 in the whole Spanish store, #1 in the whole Canadian store, #11 in the almighty US store. It's amazing!]**
- It gave me the idea to write THIS book. **[2021: And many more.]**

I can't guarantee you the same results, but if I was able to do it, why can't you?

Don't forget that it took me a year from starting writing to the first nice sum of money coming in. I had two unsuccessful promos before "the one that hit it out of the park"[and one after!].

I've been rejected by more than 30 publishers and agents and ridiculed by a couple. It was not nice, but I'm still standing. **[2021: It might have been a blessing in disguise. I doubt that I would sell the amounts of books I sell with a publisher, and I get a royalty six to seven times as high.]**

I had and still have people telling me that my book is lacking loads of stuff. Of course it's always the people who can help me fix it for a nice sum of money.
I listen to their advice, and then I do what I think is right and go with my gut feeling.

Even after taking off, there will still be struggles. And even though I'm now making five figures a month, I had to get a loan from Mum and a couple of friends last January (watch those spendings and liquidity).

Always remember, there are no mistakes in life, only lessons. If something goes wrong, search for the lesson you have to learn from it. If your plan doesn't work, change it. If the new one doesn't work either, change it again until it works.

Market your first book. There is lots of information out there.
And of course...**write a second book!** It will help to sell your first one. And then write a third book, and a fourth one, and a fifth one. The more the merrier.

Don't believe everything you hear, not even what I'm telling you. Do your own research, and do it your way!

YOU GOT THIS! GO FOR IT! [I'd say "good luck," but I don't believe in luck. I believe in hard work and agree 100% with Jack Nicklaus's quote: "The more I practice, the luckier I seem to get."
[2021: Maybe I was a little lucky. What are the odds that a Japanese translator finds your book among eight million Kindle books and gets you three publishing contracts with +75000 copies sold. But above all, I think it was because I never gave up on

myself and my books and - of course the appearance of Amazon advertising.]

The most successful authors I know have five things in common:
1) They write lots of books (at least ten, but the more the merrier).
2) They continuously promote one or more books of their backlist for free or for 99c to attract new readers.
3) They heavily invest in ads on Amazon, Facebook, and BookBub.
4) They learn how to do their own ads and don't outsource.
5) They have a business mindset. They don't see themselves as mere writers but also as business people and publishers. Adam Croft's book *The Indie Author Mindset* helped me a lot with that.

2021

Everything has changed. Thanks to Amazon ads, I now consistently sell as many books every month as before with BookBub deals once a year. So once you have a couple of books out there, you should definitely learn how to advertise your books. I'm shamelessly selling Mark Dawson's course because it changed my life. It opens twice a year. You can check it out here.

I also wish you MAGIC. That's what happens when "the universe conspires in your favor" as two of my favorites, Paulo Coelho and Ralph Waldo Emerson, say .

Expect a miracle at every corner, and with time, you'll see things happening in your life that are better than you ever imagined.

Now go finish that next book and upload it to Amazon!
To your success!
P.S. Any questions, drop me an e-mail. I'll answer.
marc@marcreklau.com

ABOUT THE AUTHOR

Marc Reklau (Esslingen am Neckar, Germany, 1973), is a life and executive coach and personal development expert. After an amazing and rewarding life journey that took him from his native country to the United States, Mexico and Spain, he finally found his calling: Coaching.

He currently spends his time running along the beach of Barcelona and coaching clients from all over the world. Marc's mission is to empower people to create the life they want and to give them the resources and tools to make it happen. He still spends 14 - 15 hours every week researching, studying and applying the principles and secrets of success and happiness.

His message is simple: Many people want to change things in their lives, but few are willing to do a simple set of exercises constantly over a period of time. You can plan and create success and happiness in your life by installing habits that support you on the way to your goal.

His first book *30 Days: Change Your Habits, Change Your Life* became an Amazon Bestseller "over night"(after one year of hard work).

After having 40,000 downloads in 72 hours, it was #2 OVERALL in the FREE Kindle Store and then hit Amazon's paid bestseller lists in its category in 7 Kindle stores worldwide, staying there for over 2 months.

If you want to hire Marc as your coach, you can directly contact him on his homepage www.marcreklau.com where you will also find more information about him and his work.

Facebook: www.facebook.com/marcreklaucoaching
Twitter: @MarcReklau
e-mail: marc@marcreklau.com

Printed in Great Britain
by Amazon